VITAMINS

Unravels the complexities of this important subject and explains in an easy-to-read style the role of vitamins in our lives, with advice on planning diet and lifestyle to ensure lasting good health.

GW00708289

VITAMINS
What They Are and Why We Need Them

by

CAROL HUNTER

NATURE'S WAY

THORSONS PUBLISHERS LIMITED
Wellingborough, Northamptonshire

First published February 1978
Second Impression December 1978
Third Impression 1979
Fourth Impression 1981

ISBN 0 7225 0407 1

Printed and bound in Great Britain by
Richard Clay (The Chaucer Press) Ltd.,
Bungay, Suffolk.

CONTENTS

CHAPTER ONE

AN INTRODUCTION TO VITAMINS

Vitamin is a common enough word these days, but most people have only the haziest idea of what the term really means. Vitamins are not just an added nutritional bonus, as some advertisements would have us believe, but are chemical substances essential not only to our health and well-being, but also to life itself.

When vitamins are under-supplied, any number of illnesses can ensue, and although severe deficiency diseases like scurvy and beri beri are rarely seen now, other less serious deficiency symptoms are widespread. Dandruff, dry skin, bruises, bleeding gums, poor eyesight are just a few of the tell-tale signs that the diet is lacking in certain vitamins.

All foods contain small quantities of vitamins, but only comparatively recently has the existence of these nutrients been established. They are a discovery of the twentieth century, for it was not until 1911 that the first of the vitamins was identified.

Before that time researchers had suspected the presence of some unidentified nutrients in food, but until the late nineteenth century little had been done to isolate the biochemical action of the various components of food. Once the first vitamin was identified, other discoveries quickly followed suit, and researchers working in several different countries made discoveries almost simultaneously as the pieces of the jigsaw began to fit together.

Vitamins of course, have always been present in food even though we were previously unaware of their existence. As early as 1753 citrus fruits were recommended for the treatment of scurvy in sailors, though it was not then known that it was their vitamin C content which produced a cure.

This debilitating disease was widespread in those days among seafaring men, who often had to exist for months on a diet lacking in fresh fruit and vegetables. Such a diet was almost completely devoid of vitamin C, and often led to a high incidence of disease and even death on long sea voyages.

Many cures were tried and rejected before it was realized that citrus fruits held the key. Some attributed scurvy to a change of air or lack of exercise, and even when citrus fruits were recognized as a cure, it was believed to be their acidity which did the trick. This led to some doctors recommending vinegar or sulphuric acid as a remedy, with disastrous results.

In 1753 Dr James Lind wrote a comprehensive study of the disease, *A Treatise of Scurvy*, and soon afterwards all Admiralty ships were instructed to carry lemons and fresh vegetables. The results were spectacular, with 1,754 cases in the naval hospital in Haslar in 1760, and only one in 1806. It was the recommendation of limes as a cure for scurvy which led to the label 'limey' being attached to British sailors.

In spite of this early exploratory work, vitamin C was not officially recognized until 1928, when it was isolated by Gyorgyi, and it was not produced chemically until 1933 when its structural formula was established.

FROM THE ROMAN DAYS

Even though Vitamin A was not discovered until 1913, cod liver oil (a rich source of vitamin A) had been used for centuries. Even in the days of the Greeks and the Romans, night blindness was alleviated by eating liver. And in 1883 a doctor on a Brazilian plantation connected poor sight among the slave population with the lack of green vegetables in their diet. The vitamin was discovered by Drs McCollum and Davis at John Hopkins University in America, when they isolated a growth factor in egg yolk and butter. Vitamin A was chemically synthesized for the first time in 1930.

ON THE TRACK OF THE B VITAMINS

Vitamin B was at first thought to be one single vitamin, and as such was identified by the Polish chemist, Casimir Funk in 1911. He extracted from rice polishings a crystalline substance which was capable of curing beri-beri, and it was to this substance that he gave the name of vitamine from the Latin 'vita', meaning life, and 'amine', meaning containing basic or 'amine nitrogen'. A year later Sir Frederick Gowland Hopkins also published a statement on the anti beri-beri vitamin, now known to be vitamin B1 or thiamine.

However, their work was preceded by that of a Dutch doctor in Java. In 1897 Eijkman discovered that polyneuritis (a disease identical to beri-beri) in fowl only occurred when they were fed on polished rice. He also found the same to be true with prison inmates but he was unable to establish just what substance was responsible.

THE DISCOVERY OF NIACIN

At the turn of the century pellagra was a common disease in the Southern States of America, and between 1915 and 1916 it ranked as the second cause of death in Carolina. Early investigations into this disease were made at the beginning of the century by Dr Joseph Goldberger.

He was sent to the South by the U.S. National Institute of Health, and in the course of his work discovered that none of the medical staff on the plantations caught the disease, although at that time it was thought to be contagious. Further investigations revealed that the staff ate a far more varied diet than did the workers, who lived mainly on corn bread, grits and fatty pork.

Goldberger came close to solving the problem, but it was not until 1937 that R.J. Madden at Wisconsin University used niacin to successfully treat pellagra. Almost simultaneously doctors in London and Egypt discovered the vitamin.

ON THE WRONG TRACK

At one time investigators had thought riboflavin to be the cure for pellagra. This vitamin was first isolated from whey, in 1879 but it was not suspected as being an essential nutrient until 1932 when it was isolated from yeast. The vitamin was first synthesized in 1935.

A LATE-COMER

Vitamin B12 is a comparatively recent addition to the B complex, its complete structure first being recognized by scientists in England and America in 1948. Early studies of what is now known to be B12 began in the 1920s, when three American doctors Minot, Murphy and Whipple examined the reasons why those suffering from anaemia no longer produced red blood corpuscles in the bone marrow. Pernicious anaemia, they decided, resulted when the intrinsic factor could not be produced because a substance (now known to be B12) was lacking.

OTHER MEMBERS OF THE B COMPLEX

Vitamin B6 was discovered in 1936 by Gyorgyi, who identified a nutritional factor which, when lacking, caused dermatitis in rats. This new factor was isolated in 1939 by several researchers, and was first synthesized in the same year.

Folic acid was discovered in 1941 during research work on a concentrate obtained from spinach. Four years later the chemical structure and synthesis of folic acid were discovered by a group of American scientists.

PABA, an integral part of folic acid, was first synthesized by Fischer in 1863, although it was not recognized as a vitamin until 1940 when it was granted inclusion in the B complex.

A substance now known to be pantothenic acid was first discovered in yeast in 1901, but it was not until 1940 that this vitamin was first recognized and synthesized by scientists in Germany, Switzerland and America.

The first knowledge of biotin was gained in 1916 when a researcher named Bateman observed that a high concentration of egg white in experimental diets proved toxic. Between 1913 and 1940 Gyorgyi and his colleagues conducted work on this substance, and by 1936 they had obtained a crystalline substance from egg yolk. In 1940 biotin was isolated from liver, and its structure established, and three years later American research scientists produced it synthetically.

Choline was first used experimentally in 1939 when it was shown to relieve a condition known as fatty liver.

In the same year inositol was accepted as a B complex vitamin, although this substance was first identified as a food factor as early as 1850. In 1940 Dr Woolley in America discovered that mice fed a diet deficient in inositol suffered from stunted growth and falling hair, and that these condition were remedied when inositol was added to their food.

A CURE FOR RICKETS

Cod liver oil was used a century ago to treat rickets, but the discovery of vitamin D was delayed because scientists thought the effective substance in the oil was vitamin A.

In 1918 Mellanby found that dogs suffering from rickets could be cured by cod liver oil, and in 1922 McCollum showed that vitamin A in other foods would not effect a cure. He went on to experiment with destroying the vitamin A in cod liver oil, and showing that this still cured rickets.

In 1919 research proved that the action of the sun's ultra violet rays also helped relieve rickets, although such a link was first suggested by Dr T.A. Palm in 1890, when he found the disease to be scarce in countries with plenty of sun. Vitamin D was not synthesized until 1935, since when about 20 different forms of the vitamin have been found although only two (D_2 and D_3) are in use.

E FOR FERTILITY

Vitamin E was first isolated from wheat germ oil in 1936, although its existence was first suspected in 1920, and in 1922 the substance was proved essential for normal reproduction. American scientists found that rats failed to reproduce when the vitamin was lacking. In 1931 it was discovered that laboratory animals developed muscular dystrophy when deprived of the substance, and in 1938 children suffering from this condition were successfully treated with vitamin E.

Vitamin F was first described in 1929 when research workers observed a fat deficiency disease in laboratory animals deprived of fatty acids in their diet.

CHICKENS HELD THE ANSWER
A disease in chickens characterized by haemorrhaging was found to be cured by fish meal in the early 1930s, and in 1934 Dam in Copenhagen suggested that this was because the meal contained a fat soluble vitamin, which he named K from the Danish word 'koagulation'. Many attempts were made to isolate this vitamin before it was finally achieved in 1939 by Dam and his colleagues.

In 1926 Gyorgyi and his co-workers discovered that a substance present in both paprika and lemon juice appeared to be superior to vitamin C in preventing capillary bleeding. This substance was named citrin, but it was later found that there was a whole family of bioflavonoids, of which rutin and hesperidin are the most active. Vitamin P was so named by Gyorgyi after the word paprika.

IN SEARCH OF VITAMINS
Since few of the vitamins can be manufactured by the body, it becomes essential to our health to obtain them from other sources. Our health and growth depend upon our taking in certain quantities of all the vitamins, and although these are present in food, it is not as simple as it sounds to obtain sufficient vitamins from our diet.

For a start, the amount of a particular vitamin in

a particular food will vary according to such factors as the time of year, the soil in which it was grown, and growing conditions. This means, of course, that any tables showing the vitamin content of foods can only be based on average figures.

Added to this, most vitamins are extremely unstable and can easily be destroyed in any of several different ways before you actually consume your food. As you will see in Chapter 10, air, light, heat, water, storage and refining are just some of the factors responsible for the destruction of vitamins.

To complicate matters further, everybody's vitamin requirements vary, to such an extent that you will even need differing amounts from someone with identical height, weight and age. Some people have a far greater need for vitamins than others. For example expectant mothers, drinkers, smokers, those under stress and old people.

This is why the government can only lay down arbitrary minimum intake levels, below which it is known ill health will ensue. Such figures are not the amounts needed to maintain any one person in optimum health, but they should be sufficient to prevent the occurrence of actual deficiency disease. And there is a world of difference between obtaining sufficient vitamins to ward off deficiency symptoms, and getting enough to enjoy good health.

By the way, the government in Britain appears to err on the side of caution when it comes to recommending minimum daily intake of vitamins.

For instance, in America the figures tend to be much higher, in fact up to double the amount listed by the British government, and some countries such as Russia and Germany advise up to four times the intake of some vitamins. It all serves to illustrate the lack of firm knowledge on the subject.

Having accepted that individual vitamin requirements differ, how do you set about ensuring that you are getting enough vitamins? Obviously food must come first, the basic principle of good nutrition being to choose your diet carefully. In the case of vitamins, this means eating lots of raw fresh fruit and vegetables, and as many unrefined foods as possible.

To make sure you are getting sufficient vitamins, you should also pay attention to the freshness of your food, and to the way you store and cook it, as detailed in Chapter 10.

TOPPING UP YOUR INTAKE

Having done all you can as far as your food is concerned – and you cannot always eat as you would wish to – you can also supplement your diet with vitamin preparations. Some people like to take a daily multi-vitamin and mineral supplement as an insurance policy to keep themselves healthy. Others tend to leave it rather too late, and do not take a vitamin supplement until they are suffering from definite deficiency symptoms.

Either way, it is important to remember that a supplement of one particular vitamin should not be taken in isolation. An individual vitamin should always be taken in conjuction with a multi-vitamin preparation. Vitamins work both individually and as a team, and taking one in isolation can create a deficiency of some of the other vitamins. It is also believed that a multi-vitamin supplement will facilitate the absorption of a single vitamin.

When it comes to choosing a supplement you are faced with two alternatives, a natural and a synthetic preparation. With most of the vitamins, chemical analysis reveals no difference between the two – although in the case of vitamin E, that which is obtained from natural sources has 36 per cent more biological potency than synthetic vitamin E.

The difference between the two forms lies in the fact that in nature vitamins never occur in isolation (as they do when reproduced chemically in the laboratory). Vitamin C, for instance, always occurs in association with the bioflavonoids, which enhance its effectiveness.

If you are wanting to take large quantities of vitamins, it is usually difficult to obtain sufficiently high dosages from natural supplements, but in general it seems to be worth paying slightly more for them rather than the synthetic versions.

Vitamins fall roughly into two different groups; namely those that are soluble in water and those soluble in fat. You will find that as a rule the water soluble vitamins (B and C) are declared by weight and expressed in milligrams or micrograms. The fat soluble vitamins, on the other hand, tend to be measured by activity and declared in international units, a measurement established by the United Nations.

The subject of vitamins is an extremely complex and confusing one – but it is also one of extreme importance to everybody concerned with their own health. This book does not attempt to blind you with science, or to record technical details of complicated trials. Instead, it aims to give you a basic understanding of the importance of vitamins, and to assist you in planning your diet and lifestyle so that you may enjoy lasting good health.

CHAPTER TWO

VITAMIN A

he eyes are usually the first part of the body to be
ffected if your diet is short of vitamin A – and
eficiencies of this vitamin are more common
han of any other vitamin.

Difficulty in adjusting to sudden changes in
ght, or an inability to see properly in the dark,
ould mean your diet is lacking sufficient
uantities of this vitamin.

Correct vision is closely related to vitamin A
ntake, and night vision depends entirely on an
mple supply of the vitamin. This is because a
ubstance in the eyes called visual purple is used
p as light reaches the eyes, and since this is
ormed from vitamin A and protein, it cannot be
eplaced immediately if the vitamin is in short

supply. Hence the time gap before you can adjust fully to sudden changes in light.

For the same reason, anybody who uses his eyes a lot (such as typists or draughtsmen), who works in dim or artificial light, or who watches a lot of television, will require extra vitamin A to replace that which is used up.

While a shortage of vitamin A often causes itchy or burning eyes, over-sensitivity to light, styes, or mucus in the eyes, there are other sure signs of a deficiency. The skin suffers too, with clogged pores often leading to whiteheads, pimples and other blemishes, while rough skin resembling goose flesh appears on the backs of the arms, the knees and thighs. Dandruff and a dry, itchy scalp are often associated with a vitamin A deficiency and so are brittle, peeling finger nails.

THE VITAMIN'S OTHER ROLES

Vitamin A has another important function to perform in maintaining the health of the linings of the body cavities, such as the nose, throat, mouth, sinuses, bronchial tubes, lungs, bladder, stomach etc. When these are healthy they are covered with a layer of mucus which washes them clean and prevents invasion by bacterial infection.

However, with a shortage of vitamin A, the cells lining these cavities grow too rapidly and dead cells accumulate, becoming thick and scaly instead of covered with mucus. This medium is an ideal breeding ground for bacteria, and an number of infections may result, the most common being respiratory complaints.

Vitamin A is associated with vitamin D (the two

often occur in the same foods), and they share a common role in being essential for normal growth, bone structure and tooth enamel. This makes an adequate intake of both vitamins particularly important for growing children.

An equally important point in this day and age is that vitamin A combines with vitamin E in protecting the body from the ravages of air pollution. This is accomplished by the mucous membranes filtering out dust and toxic substances, but in the course of this process vitamin A is used up, thereby increasing the body's need for the vitamin under these conditions.

Animal tests in America have suggested that vitamin A can also inhibit certain cancer growths, but this is still in the very early stages of research.

WHERE TO FIND VITAMIN A

We obtain our vitamin A from food in two different forms. Some of it we get directly, and some is supplied in the form of carotene, or pro-vitamin A, which the body is able to convert in the liver to vitamin A.

The richest sources of vitamin A are fish liver oils, butter, milk, egg yolks and fish (especially when canned in oil). The quantity of vitamin A found in dairy produce varies considerably, being almost twice as high during the summer months when pastures are greener.

Carotene is so named because it was first discovered in carrots – the old wives' tale about carrots helping you to see in the dark is really true! This yellowish pigment is found in most yellow or dark green fruits and vegetables, being most plentiful in apricots, watercress, parsley, oranges, peaches, melons, carrots and marrow. The darker the colour of such a plant, the more carotene it contains.

The body has some difficulty in absorbing carotene from foods, because this substance is enclosed in cellulose cell walls which we are unable to digest. These walls must first be broken down or softened by mechanical means (e.g. grating or chopping), by cooking, or by chewing.

Studies have shown that the carotene absorbed from vegetables is between 16 and 35 per cent, the amount being greater in vegetables of softer texture. As little as one per cent may be absorbed from raw carrots, the figure increasing to between 5 and 19 per cent for cooked carrots. Some people, such as diabetics, may also have difficulty in converting carotene to vitamin A.

A FAT SOLUBLE VITAMIN

Being one of the fat soluble vitamins, vitamin A can be stored in the body. Approximately 90 per cent of that retained is stored in the liver, with small quantities in the kidneys and the lungs. Carotene, too, is stored in the liver and in the fatty tissues below the skin.

Before the body can make use of either vitamin A or carotene, sufficient fat must be present. This is why a supplement, if taken, should follow a meal containing some fat. Vitamin A and carotene must combine with bile salts in the intestine before they can pass into the blood and be conveyed to the liver. When there is insufficien at, little or no bile reaches the intestines, and almost all the vitamin A and carotene is lost by excretion.

Also necessary for proper utilization of vitamin A are adequate quantities of protein, vitamin E and zinc. Vitamin E also prevents the destruction of vitamin A in the body.

HOW MUCH WE NEED

The daily intake recommended in Britain (remembering that this is the minimum required to ward off ill health) is 2,500 i.u.'s for adults, or half that amount for children under 12 years old. As with several other vitamins, this is a mere half of the intake recommended in America.

In old age, quantities double the above are advisable, but it is not generally a good idea to exceed 5,000 i.u.'s a day except for therapeutic purposes. The need for vitamin A also increases under conditions of stress, or in diseases of the liver, kidneys, intestines or respiratory tract.

Because it can be stored by the body, vitamin A is one of those vitamins which can prove toxic if taken in excessive quantities. This need be of no concern to most people, since any toxic effects are only likely to develop if quantities over 50,000 i.u.'s are taken every day for long periods of time. That would mean eating an awful lot of carrots, or swallowing handsful of tablets!

The symptoms of toxicity (lack of appetite, nausea, swelling, and aching bones) disappear as soon as the vitamin is discontinued. An excess of carotene is also unlikely, and this has no serious toxic reaction, although it can produce slight yellowing of the skin.

Vitamin A and carotene are both relatively stable, although they can be destroyed by frying, by a combination of oxygen and heat, and by nitrates and nitrites which are widely used as fertilizers and food preservatives. Dried foods often contain as little as half the vitamin A that they would have done in their fresh state.

CHAPTER THREE

THE VITAMIN B COMPLEX

Vitamin B is the most complicated of the vitamins, comprising not just one but 13 different types. While each individual member of the vitamin B complex has a separate function to perform, the B vitamins are also inter-related and inter-dependent. It is therefore not surprising to find that these vitamins are all present in the same foods, the best sources being liver, brewer's yeast, wheat germ, whole grains and molasses.

Considered as a whole, the B complex is responsible for maintaining mental health, and for the health of the nervous system, the digestion and the skin. It is unlikely that you will suffer from a deficiency of just one member of the complex, although the deficiency symptoms of any particular member may be most prominent.

As a rule, if you are short of one B vitamin you are short of the others too, which is why any supplement of an individual B vitamin should be accompanied by a supplement providing the other vitamins of the B complex. This is very important, since taking one B vitamin in isolation may increase the body's need for other members of the complex.

This delicate balance of the B complex tends to be upset by modern food refining methods, which often destroy several of the B vitamins. A good example of this is white flour – during its manufacture five of the B vitamins are almost totally destroyed, but only two of this number are added back in synthetic form to the end product.

SPOTTING A DEFICIENCY

A well-known American writer on nutrition, Adelle Davis, maintained that the tongue is a good indicator of whether or not you are lacking the B vitamins. The tongue should be moderate in size, pink in colour, smooth-textured and uncoated, with a uniform distribution of taste buds. She believed that any variation from this norm was suggestive of a vitamin B deficiency – but she also added that she had found it extremely rare to come across a tongue in such good condition.

Other common symptoms of a lack of vitamin B are tiredness, depression, irritability and nervousness as well as acne or other skin problems, poor appetite and digestion, and greying or falling hair.

Both sugar and alcohol use up the B vitamins, and since the B complex is concerned with the production of energy, the more exercise, work or stress you are faced with, the more B vitamins you will need.

The vitamin B complex is water soluble, and because of this most of the B vitamins are easily destroyed by such factors as heat and water. Since most members of the complex cannot be stored in the body there is no danger of toxicity, and any excess is lost through excretion.

THIAMINE – VITAMIN B1

Thiamine, or vitamin B1, was the first of the B vitamins to be discovered, and researchers initially thought it to be the only one in existence.

Thiamine is the most vulnerable of the B vitamins and so a deficiency is particularly common. It is especially vulnerable to heat, and is also destroyed by refining, exposure to air, water, and alkalis such as baking powder.

To give you an idea of how easily thiamine is destroyed, up to 50 per cent is lost in cooking water, and 15 per cent is lost during baking – a figure which doubles if baking soda is used. Toasting bread destroys a further 15 per cent for thick slices, or up to 30 per cent for thin slices.

Early signs of a thiamine deficiency are common but are difficult to detect since they include such symptoms as fatigue, insomnia, headaches, indigestion, poor appetite, alternating constipation and diarrhoea, depression, emotional instability, and nerve troubles.

If a deficiency is allowed to progress, it will

eventually lead to beri-beri, a debilitating disease frequently seen in Eastern countries where a diet with a heavy emphasis on polished rice means thiamine is in short supply (only the unpolished rice contains the vitamin). Beri-beri is characterized by paralysis and general debility, heart trouble, and breathing difficulties.

THE ROLE OF THIAMINE

As can be seen from the early deficiency symptoms mentioned above, thiamine's main concern is with the nerves and the digestion. Both of these systems suffer when thiamine is insufficient to perform its most important role which lies in assisting in the conversion of starches and sugars to energy. When thiamine is in short supply, neither the nerves nor the brain can derive sufficient energy to operate efficiently.

At the same time, thiamine helps to maintain muscle tone in the digestive tract, and to control the stomach's secretion of hydrochloric acid which is essential for proper digestion and elimination. Because thiamine's main role is in assisting in the metabolism of carbohydrates, it follows that the more starches and sugars your diet contains, the more thiamine your body needs.

Increased needs for thiamine also exist during pregnancy and breast-feeding, or in any digestive or liver disturbance. Alcohol interferes with the body's use of thiamine (alcoholics or heavy drinkers frequently suffer from a deficiency), and both sugar and smoking deplete this vitamin.

The richest source of thiamine is brewer's yeast

followed by wheat germ and unprocessed cereals. Other foods containing a reasonable amount of this vitamin are the pulse foods (lentils, haricot beans etc.), egg yolk, liver and nuts.

The recommended minimum daily intake in Britain is 0.8 to 1.4 mg for adults, or 0.3 to 1 mg for children up to 12 years old.

RIBOFLAVIN – VITAMIN B2

The skin and the eyes are usually affected when riboflavin or vitamin B2 is in short supply. The skin becomes cracked and rough, and acne, dermatitis or eczema may develop. The eyes become bloodshot and prone to watering, while being extremely sensitive to light. It becomes difficult to see in dim light, and a lack of this vitamin has even been linked with cataracts.

Riboflavin is less important to mental health than the other B vitamins, but nervous symptoms such as shaking, muscular weakness and dizziness may occur with a deficiency. Like thiamine, this vitamin is concerned with the conversion of fats, protein and sugars into energy, and as such it is essential for normal growth and tissue maintenance.

Light is capable of destroying large quantities of riboflavin. For instance, if you leave a bottle of milk sitting on a sunny doorstep for as little as three hours, it will have lost 70 per cent of its riboflavin content! Water and heat also destroy this vitamin, as they do other members of the B complex. The body sometimes experiences difficulty in absorbing riboflavin, for instance if insufficient hydrochloric acid is secreted, or if the mineral phosphorus is lacking.

Yeast, milk, liver and leafy green vegetables are the best dietary sources of riboflavin, but it is also present in bran, wheat germ, wholegrain cereals, heart, veal, chicken, apricots, tomatoes, tea and beer (which should not be taken as a licence to drink vast quantities!) The British recommended minimum daily intake is 1.3 to 1.7 mg for adults, or 0.4 to 1.2 mg for children.

NIACIN – VITAMIN B3

There has been excitement in recent years over the successful use of niacin in treating cases of schizophrenia. Trials conducted over a number of years in Canada indicated a 70 to 80 per cent success rate when large quantities of the vitamin were administered (see page 88).

Niacin, which is also known as niacinamide, nicotinic acid, or nicotinamide, is essential for proper brain functioning, and a deficiency may be marked by tension, depression and instability. But while psychological changes are usually the first to be noted, digestive disturbances also occur with a deficiency because the secretion of hydrochloric acid decreases, leading to either constipation or diarrhoea, and flatulence, nausea or vomiting, coated tongue and bad breath.

Like the B vitamins already discussed, niacin assists in the breakdown and utilization of fats, protein and carbohydrates. It has also been found to assist migraine sufferers, to relieve the pain of arthritis, and to benefit alcoholics when given in large doses of between 3 and 20 grammes daily.

Niacin was first discovered when pellagra, now

known to be a deficiency disease, was investigated (see page 11). This disease, from the Italian meaning for 'rough skin' was common among people living predominantly on a maize diet, and it is described as 'the three d's': diarrhoea, dermatitis, and dementia; leading finally to a fourth d – destruction of the nervous system.

Unlike most of the vitamins in the B complex, the body is able to form small quantities of niacin. This it achieves by conversion of the amino acid tryptophan (one of the constituents of protein), but only when protein and the vitamins riboflavin and B6 are in ample supply.

Niacin is destroyed in water, and taking certain drugs, such as antibiotics, may also create a deficiency. If a supplement of niacin is taken, some people experience a temporary flushing, caused by dilating of the blood vessels, but this may be avoided by taking the vitamin in a modified form.

Good dietary sources of niacin are liver, lean meat, fish, brewer's yeast and wheat germ. Smaller quantities are also found in eggs, wholemeal bread, nuts, bran and beer. The recommended minimum daily intake in the U.K. for this vitamin is 15-18 mg for adults, and 5-14 mg for children.

VITAMIN B6 – PYRIDOXINE

The more protein your diet contains (i.e. meat, fish, eggs and dairy produce), the more vitamin B6 you need. This is because B6, or pyridoxine as it is also known, helps the body to assimilate proteins.

Vitamin B6 has a part to play in maintaining the health of the muscular tissues, the nerves and the skin. A deficiency is therefore characterized by cardiovascular diseases, nerve troubles, skin lesions, dizziness and headaches. Since B6 is also involved in the formulation of haemoglobin (which transports oxygen in the blood), anaemia may result from a shortage of this vitamin.

Early morning sickness, which afflicts as many as half of all pregnant women, often responds to supplements of B6, sometimes accompanied by zinc.

Vitamin B6 has to be present before the body can convert the amino acid tryptophan to niacin, and before the liver can synthesize lecithin, the substance which helps prevent the build up of fats and cholesterol.

When infants obtain insufficient B6 they may suffer from convulsions – this was learned the hard way when a bottle formula without this vitamin was widely used. The vitamin also acts as a diuretic by ridding the body of excess fluid.

Although B6 is widely distributed in foods, much is lost by canning, cooking, light, heat, and long storage. The foods to choose for a good B6 intake are bran, wheat germ, wholegrains, liver, brewer's yeast, brown rice, meat, milk, peas, pulses (lentils, haricot beans etc.), and peanuts. Although the British government issues no recommended intake for this vitamin, it is thought to be in the region of 1 mg for adults, and 0.5 mg for children.

VITAMIN B12

Those who do not eat meat are the ones most likely to suffer from a deficiency of vitamin B12, since this vitamin is well supplied in meats (especially liver and kidneys), but occurs in virtually no plants. Fortunately for vegetarians who wish to augment their intake by using a supplement, manufacturers can now obtain the vitamin from non-animal sources by using a mould.

Less is known about B12 (or cyanocobalamine to give it its scientific name) than the other B vitamins, since it was only discovered in 1948, and comparatively little research has yet been done on it. The vitamin is known to contain cobalt, making it the only vitamin with a mineral element.

Pernicious anaemia, in which the nerve cells are injured, is the disease most commonly associated with a serious lack of this vitamin. In the absence of B12 the stomach is unable to produce an enzyme known as the intrinsic factor, without which new red blood cells cannot be formed.

Like the other B vitamins, mental disturbances, digestive problems and nerve troubles are also connected with a deficiency of B12. These are characterized by such deficiency symptoms as loss of appetite and weight, impaired memory, fatigue, shortness of breath and loss of hair. B12 is also thought to be involved in the utilization of protein, fats and carbohydrates, along with other members of the B complex.

Some B12 can be stored in the body, principally in the liver which, if in a good state, may hold sufficient to last as long as three years. This is not surprising when you consider that B12 appears to be needed in only a fraction of the amount of other B vitamins. It is measured in micrograms rather than milligrams, and while the exact amount needed has not been established, it is thought to be in the region of 1-5 mcg for adults, or 0.5-1 mcg for children.

Vitamin B12 is destroyed by light and by strong acid or alkaline solutions. Since it is closely associated with folic acid – another of the B complex – the two should be taken together when a supplement is considered.

FOLIC ACID

Folic acid is richest in deep green leafy vegetables, and it is this association with foliage which gives the vitamin its name. Other good sources in the diet are liver, kidneys, and brewer's yeast.

As has just been mentioned, folic acid is closely linked with vitamin B12, and the two are needed for production of normal red blood cells. If both are in short supply blood cells do not mature and divide, but increase in size and get fewer in number – a condition known as megaloblastic anaemia. It is not advisable to take folic acid in isolation, since it tends to mask a vitamin B12 deficiency.

A mild deficiency of folic acid is thought to be quite common, and is especially frequent among pregnant women since the need for this vitamin doubles in the last three months of pregnancy. Folic acid is essential to normal brain functioning and a deficiency can cause irritability, forgetfulness, and mental sluggishness. Should this be prolonged, mental deterioration may occur, and a lack is commonly found among mental patients. As many as 90 per cent of alcoholics are said to suffer from a deficiency since their bodies cannot absorb folic acid.

The nerves and the digestion are other areas of the body which suffer in cases of a shortage of this vitamin. Because folic acid is necessary for the division of all body cells, proper development is also impaired.

Light and heat cause deterioration of folic acid, as does long storage, especially at room temperature; and cooking may destroy as much as 50 to 90 per cent. That which reaches the body is protected by vitamin C from disintegration and oxidation. The daily requirement of folic acid is thought to be around 0.4 mg.

PABA

PABA stands for a tongue-twisting name – para-aminobenzoic acid. This is in fact a component of folic acid, although it is usually classified as an individual B vitamin.

PABA is important for normal growth, for the health of the skin and the intestines. Those who would like to restore colour to grey hair will be interested to know that greying has been linked with a deficiency of PABA. Persevering with a supplement of PABA for six months (with increased quantities of copper, folic acid and pantothenic acid) is said to restore some colour to grey hair in 70 per cent of cases, although this should perhaps be viewed with mild scepticism! The recommended amount for those who wish to take the cure' is 200 mg after each meal.

PABA also acts as a screen against the burning rays of the sun, an ability which has earned it a place in some suntan preparations. Its presence in creams and ointments also helps in healing eczema and other skin complaints.

Liver, yeast and wheat germ are the best sources of PABA, but some may also be synthesized by bacteria in the intestines. It has not yet been established how much PABA is needed by the body.

PANTOTHENIC ACID

Pantothenic acid is involved in many different body processes, although it is most commonly referred to as the stress vitamin, since it builds up a resistance to both mental stress, and stress in the form of infections.

The adrenal glands which regulate many of the body processes depend upon a sufficient quantity of pantothenic acid, and when it is in poor supply their exhaustion can lead to muscle weakness, fatigue, and lack of hydrochloric acid (thereby impairing digestion).

Although a deficiency of this vitamin is believed to be fairly rare, symptoms include depression, nerve disorders, mental symptoms, indigestion, loss of appetite, baldness and greying hair.

Pantothenic acid is also involved in the production of energy from fats, starch and protein, and is needed to maintain proper levels of blood sugar in the body, and for the use of cholesterol and other fatty substances.

Recent research has suggested that the

common and crippling disease of arthritis may result from a deficiency disease due to lack of this vitamin. A British doctor, E.C. Barton-Wright, who has conducted extensive research and trials on this subject, is convinced that if everybody had a daily intake of 25-30 mg of pantothenic acid (considerably higher than the average), arthritis would be virtually wiped out.

He has found that arthritics have only half the blood level of pantothenic acid of healthy patients, and he has achieved considerable success in treating sufferers with large doses of the vitamin (in the region of 4 grammes daily) in a special form of injection. Calcium pantothenate supplements taken in this quantity have sometimes achieved similar results, but improvement is often slow because the damaged adrenal glands take time to repair themselves.

Pantothenic acid is present in all living cells, and so is well distributed in foods, even though it is found only in small quantities. The best sources are brewer's yeast, liver, wheat germ, peas, soyabeans, peanuts, meat, fish and wholegrains. This vitamin is unstable when in contact with heat and losses ranging from from 15 to 56 per cent occur in canning, heat drying or cooking. The milling of wheat causes a loss of 50 per cent.

The minimum daily intake is thought to be between 5 and 10 mg for adults, or about 2.5 mg for children.

BIOTIN

Biotin is grouped with the B vitamins, although it is sometimes known as vitamin H. It is only needed by the body in very small quantities (˙ mcg daily for adults, or 0.25 mcg for children), and since it is widely distributed in food a deficiency i rare. Where this does occur it is likely to resul from the use of antibiotics, which destroy biotin.

Symptoms of such a deficiency are similar t those for thiamine, namely muscular pain, poo appetite, dry skin, disturbed nervous system, ski troubles and lack of energy.

Biotin is thought to assist in the synthesis c haemoglobin, and in the manufacture c glycogen, our means of storing energy in the live

Small quantities of biotin are present in a animal and plant tissues, but the best dietar sources are brewer's yeast, liver, kidneys, eg yolk, milk, peas, molasses and wholegrain cereal Added to this, the intestinal bacteria are able t synthesize some biotin.

Food refining destroys some biotin, and ra egg white prevents the body absorbing it. This because the raw white contains a substance calle avidin, which binds with the biotin in such a wa as to prevent its absorption in the intestine. He generated during the cooking of the eg deactivates the avidin, but it is anyway unlike that sufficient quantities of raw egg would h consumed to cause a biotin deficiency.

CHOLINE
Preventing the accumulation of fats ar cholesterol in the body is the main function choline. Without sufficient of this B vitamin, fa accumulate in the liver, thus impairing i function, and are not converted to a suitable for

for circulation around the body.

Choline, together with inositol and B6, is also needed in sufficient quantity before the liver can manufacture lecithin, which serves a similar function to that of choline in emulsifying, or breaking down, fats. The myelin sheath which surrounds and protects the nerves is dependent upon choline, and this vitamin is also needed for normal muscle function. This is because it helps form the fluid between the nerve cells and the muscles, via which messages are relayed from the brain.

Choline is needed in comparatively large amounts (thought to be 10 mg a day for adults, or 2.5 mg for children), but some can be formed in the digestive tract from the protein amino acid methionine, provided sufficient B12 and folic acid are present. The richest source of choline is lecithin (see page 83), while other good sources are wheat germ, liver, kidneys, egg yolks and brewer's yeast.

More of this vitamin is needed when alcohol is taken, and the requirement is also dependent upon the amount of saturated fats eaten, the amounts increasing correspondingly.

INOSITOL

Inositol is associated with choline, and the two together have been shown to lower cholesterol levels in patients suffering from high accumulations. This vitamin, too, aids in fat metabolism, and is a constituent of lecithin.

Inositol is widely distributed in the body, but the highest concentrations are to be found in the muscles of the heart, in the brain and the eyes. The vitamin affects the skin and the muscular tissue, and its sedative effect helps insomnia and anxiety. A lack of inositol is also said to result in baldness, and when taken with the other B vitamins inositol is credited with stimulating hair growth.

The body is thought to need inositol in the same quantities as choline (i.e. 10 mg daily for adults, or 2.5 mg for children). A large amount of the vitamin is derived from lecithin, liver, brewer's yeast, wheat germ, oatmeal, molasses and fresh fruits, but some of it is destroyed during the course of food processing.

For the lesser known members of the vitamin B complex – vitamins B15 and B17 – see Chapter 7.

CHAPTER FOUR

VITAMIN C

More publicity has been given to vitamin C than to any other vitamin. Just about everybody recognizes oranges and blackcurrants as being good sources, and food manufacturers employ the vitamin to give their products both an added nutritional bonus, and a longer shelf life.

A fact that is less well known is that sufficient vitamin C is difficult to obtain from today's diet. Animal foods contain very little of the vitamin, the richest sources being fresh fruit and vegetables, of which many people eat too little.

The biggest handicap in obtaining sufficient vitamin C, however, is the fact that the vitamin is extremely unstable. Oxygen, light, heat and water all cause losses of vitamin C, as does the use of

baking soda, keeping foods hot, or taking such
common drugs as aspirin, barbiturates, and
antihistamines (used in the treatment of allergies).
Smoking, too, destroys vitamin C, and it has been
claimed that each cigarette smoked uses up 25
mg, or the equivalent of one orange. Any kind of
stress, whether it be an argument, extremes of
temperature, fatigue or illness, also depletes
vitamin C.

Add to this the fact that vitamin C cannot be
stored in the body, and you begin to realize that
maintaining your vitamin C level is not as simple
as eating an orange a day.

WHY WE NEED VITAMIN C

Although scientists do not believe they have yet
established all the functions of vitamin C (or
ascorbic acid, as it is also called), this vitamin has
been shown to have many important roles to play
in the maintenance of health.

The connective tissue which holds together all
the body cells depends upon an ample supply of
vitamin C, and when there is a serious deficiency
the structure of this tissue breaks down. This leads
to blood seeping from the capillaries, giving rise
to nose bleeds, thread veins, bleeding gums and a
tendency to bruise easily (all of these are early
warning signs that you are short of vitamin C).

At the same time the bone structure suffers
because the minerals calcium and phosphorus
can no longer be laid down in the bones, since
the collagen (the protein in connective tissue
and bone) is too weak to hold them. This means
that broken bones will be slow to mend, as will

any kind of wound.

Muscles and ligaments become weak too (and may even be paralysed), while teeth become loose, gums become inflamed, and anaemia may occur, along with aching joints and limbs.

All these symptoms were common enough in the past when scurvy, now known to be a vitamin C deficiency disease, was the scourge of seafaring men. It took many years before it was realized that adding citrus fruits to the diet of men at sea would keep scurvy at bay. The disease is extremely rare these days, and it has been established that a daily intake of vitamin C as low as 25 mg is sufficient to prevent its occurrence.

Vitamin C also helps in the absorption of iron, a mineral which the body has difficulty in making use of. At the same time, vitamin C acts as a detoxicant, and as such helps the body to cope with allergies (if taken in sufficient quantities, the vitamin counteracts the harmful effect of allergens in the body). Similarly, it helps the body to repel toxins, and assists in mobilizing heavy metals like copper, lead and mercury so that they can be excreted.

Vitamin C also helps to combat the dangers of nitrates and nitrites, which are widely used as food preservatives (in such foods as cheeses, processed meats and sausages). It does this by preventing the nitrates from combining with other substances in the body to produce cancer-forming nitrosamines.

OTHER USES FOR VITAMIN C
Recent research in this country suggests that

vitamin C also has a part to play in regulating cholesterol levels. Dr Constance Spittle, who conducted research on this aspect of vitamin C, found that one gramme of the vitamin taken daily lowered serum cholesterol levels in healthy patients. In those suffering from atherosclerosis (hardening of the arteries), however, she found that the levels of cholesterol in the blood increased. This she attributed to mobilization of cholesterol build up in the arteries.

Vitamin C may also benefit schizophrenics (see Chapter 12) since it has frequently been found that those suffering from this illness display a vitamin C deficiency. This is thought to be a result of the high copper levels found in schizophrenics, since copper destroys vitamin C in the body.

Any kind of infection increases the body's need for vitamin C, since at these times it disappears completely from the blood and the urine. When large doses of the vitamin are taken it has been found that many illnesses can become less severe, although in this respect vitamin C is most widely acclaimed as a means of preventing and curing the common cold.

This was a theory first propounded in America by Nobel prize winner, Dr Linus Pauling, who maintains that taking around 2 grammes of vitamin C per day will reduce both the number of colds and their severity. He recommends that at the first sign of a cold, 500 mg should be taken, a dose which is then repeated every few hours while symptoms persist.

Pauling's claim has excited much controversy on both sides of the Atlantic, but while many

experiments have been conducted, there is still
no conclusive proof to back him up. Tests in
Glasgow, Dublin, and Toronto, have confirmed
Pauling's findings, but there have also been those
that seem to refute it. Such tests have failed,
claims Pauling, because insufficient doses were
used, or because the cold virus was introduced
into the body by injection. While the controversy
continues, many people swear by vitamin C's
ability to ward off colds if high doses are taken at
the first signs of a sniffle.

A SECOND DEBATE

The question of the cold cure is not the only
controversy to have arisen over vitamin C.
Scientists are still arguing over just how much of
the vitamin we need. The minimum levels
recommended by the Department of Health in
Britain (30 mg for adults, or 20 mg for children) are
the lowest of all, with figures double this in
America, or four times as high in Russia and some
other countries.

The argument centres around the fact that
many people maintain that the optimum level of
vitamin C in the body is that at which the tissues
are saturated. This state is reached before any of
the vitamin is excreted, and those animals which
can manufacture their own vitamin C maintain
their tissues at saturation level. (Man is one of the
few animals unable to synthesize vitamin C, in
common with guinea pigs, apes and a few rare
species).

Dr Pauling recommends a regular daily intake
of between 1 and 2 grammes, and bearing in mind

how unstable the vitamin is, there would certainly
seem to be something to be said for exceeding
the paltry 30 mg advised by the Department of
Health in Britain. Large doses of vitamin C are not
toxic, since the body will excrete any excess.
Massive doses may occasionally cause diarrhoea
and, as the vitamin is a natural diuretic, the
bladder may work overtime.

Large quantities of vitamin C in natural
supplements are hard to come by and, where
greatly increased amounts are required, it may be
necessary to use a synthetic supplement. For
normal use, though, a natural supplement is to be
preferred, since in nature this vitamin occurs in
conjunction with other naturally occurring
elements such as vitamin P (see page 58).

DIETARY SOURCES OF VITAMIN C

Apart from oranges and blackcurrants, other rich
sources of vitamin C are rosehips, citrus fruit,
strawberries, green peppers and tomatoes.
Potatoes do not contain large quantities, but
because of the amount eaten they are often a
major source of the vitamin in the British diet,
provided they are carefully cooked (see page 77).
Dried peas and beans contain no vitamin C, but
when sprouted, half a cupful contains the
equivalent of six glasses of orange juice (see page
84 for instructions on sprouting).

Freshly harvested plants are richest in vitamin C
and there is a substantial loss during lengthy
storage. For instance, new potatoes in the summer
supply 30 mg per 100 g, but by March the following year this figure has fallen to only 8 mg per
100 g.

CHAPTER FIVE

VITAMIN D

Basking in the sun may produce a rich golden tan (or a red blotchy skin!), but sunbathing has another useful role to perform.

Exposing the skin to the sun enables the ultraviolet rays to react on the skin's surface oils to produce vitamin D. This is accomplished by activating a pro-vitamin, thus allowing vitamin D to pass into the body cells. The result is not achieved unless you 'strip off', since an intervening layer of clothing, or of glass, impedes the production of vitamin D. Similarly, bathing or swimming before you sit in the sun hinders the process by washing off the skin's natural oils.

Those with fair skins are able to manufacture more vitamin D in this way than those with dark skins, since more of the sun's ultra-violet rays are able to penetrate fairer skins (between 53 and 72 per cent, compared with 3 to 36 per cent for dark skins). This is one reason why immigrants in the relatively sunless climate of Britain often suffer from a vitamin D deficiency.

VITAMIN D IN THE DIET

For those who do not obtain sufficient sun – and this is a common problem in the British climate, especially among invalids or the elderly who are confined to the home – vitamin D must be derived from dietary sources.

This vitamin, however, is found in small quantities and in few foods, the only reliable sources being eggs, butter, oily fish, margarine and dried milk powder (the last two being fortified). The richest source is cod liver oil, which also supplies vitamin A. The amount of vitamin D to be found in dairy produce depends upon the time of the year, the quantity being higher during the summer months.

The vitamin D produced by the action of the sun on the skin, and that present in food, are in fact two different kinds of the same vitamin, known respectively as D_2 and D_3. Both have the same function in the body.

THE ROLE OF VITAMIN D

Vitamin D's prime role is the part it plays in bone formation, making an adequate intake especially vital for pregnant women and growing children. Babies, whether breast-fed or bottle-fed, should receive additional vitamin D since neither breastmilk nor ready-made formulas contain sufficient of the vitamin for a baby's needs.

Vitamin D must be present before calcium and phosphorus can be absorbed through the walls of the intestines to the blood, from where they are laid down in the bones. Where the vitamin is in short supply, these minerals are lost from the body by excretion. In children this can lead to rickets, a disease which is rarely seen these days, although it was widespread in all European countries up to the turn of the century.

In adults a poor supply of vitamin D may lead to osteomalacia, which is similar to rickets, while in the elderly the high incidence of osteoporosis (in which the bones become porous and inclined to fracture) is attributed to insufficient vitamin D.

Vitamin D is also needed for proper formation of the teeth, and a deficiency appears to be linked with dental decay, although this has not yet been proved conclusively. The vitamin also protects against muscle weakness, and helps to counteract cramp, insomnia, sensitivity to pain and nose bleeds.

At the same time, the vitamin assists in the release of energy within the body. The mineral phosphorus transports blood sugar through the intestinal wall and to the liver, where it is stored as glycogen. It is the burning of this glycogen which produces energy, but when the vitamin is undersupplied, the phosphorus is unable to combine with the blood sugar.

HOW TO TAKE VITAMIN D

Vitamin D is one of the fat soluble vitamins and, as

such, sufficient fat must be present before the vitamin can be absorbed from the intestines. For this reason it is advisable to take a supplement in an oily form (such as cod liver oil), or to accompany it by a meal containing some fat.

Like vitamin A, vitamin D can be toxic if taken in very large quantities, although normally a deficiency is more likely to occur than an overdose. This vitamin is stored in the liver until required by the body. An excessive intake produces such symptoms as nausea, poor appetite, vomiting, cramp, dizziness, pains, tingling fingers and toes, and excessive urine.

In more severe cases, which are of course even more unlikely, kidney damage or calcium deposits in the arteries may occur.

Toxicity has been found to result when daily doses of between 10,000 and 50,000 i.u.'s are taken over a prolonged period of time. When you compare this with the minimum daily intake recommended in Britain (250 i.u.'s for children and 100 i.u.'s for adults), you can see the unlikelihood of toxicity resulting. If toxicity symptoms were to occur though, these could quickly be removed by stopping the intake. Taking sufficient quantities of vitamins A, C and choline (one of the B vitamins) also helps to counteract toxicity.

As a fat soluble vitamin, vitamin D is fairly stable and is comparatively resistant to heat and cooking processes.

CHAPTER SIX

VITAMIN E

Vitamin E has won itself a better reputation than it probably deserves. Even in the absence of scientific proof, the vitamin has been credited with all sorts of miraculous properties – like the ability to increase virility, and to remove wrinkles and stretch marks. But, while the exact roles of this vitamin have yet to be established, there does seem to be at least some foundation for the claims made for this vitamin.

IMPROVED CIRCULATION
This vitamin is linked in many people's minds with heart disease and circulatory troubles, since an increased intake has sometimes been found helpful in treating these conditions. This stems

from what appears to be vitamin E's main function, namely acting as an antioxidant to protect polyunsaturated fats and other fatty substances from being destroyed in the body by oxygen. The substances it protects in this way include vitamin A, carotene, and the pituitary, adrenal and sex hormones.

Because vitamin E is itself destroyed in performing its role as an antioxidant, increased amounts of the vitamin are required where the diet is high in unsaturated fats. Anybody substituting vegetable fats for animal fats in the interests of health should therefore see that such a change is accompanied by an increased intake of vitamin E. The amount needed is thought to be in the region of 100 i.u.'s extra for each tablespoonful of unsaturated oil.

Vitamin E has also been found to relieve coronary thrombosis, angina, rheumatic heart disease and other allied conditions. This is because the vitamin decreases the body's need for oxygen, while at the same time increasing the supply of oxygen to the heart (and to other muscles). The vitamin's ability to reduce the amount of oxygen needed by the body's tissues also assists in cases of diabetes, threatened miscarriage, or any physical or emotional strain which may create breathing problems.

Vitamin E has also been shown to dissolve fresh clots of blood, and to bypass old ones by dilating the blood vessels, and thereby improving the circulation of blood around the body. In this capacity, the vitamin is invaluable in the treatment of varicose veins.

Where there is a deficiency of vitamin E, both the blood vessels and the muscles suffer. Muscles become weakened, often resulting in cramp, while the red blood cells deteriorate and cannot be replaced quickly enough.

THE 'SEX VITAMIN'

The manufacturers of vitamin E must have made a fortune from the widespread belief that vitamin E (the 'sex vitamin' as it is sometimes called) can improve virility if taken in large amounts. This has yet to be scientifically confirmed although, as mentioned above, sufficient quantities of the vitamin are essential to glandular function, including the production of the sex hormones. Certainly many people swear by vitamin E's ability in this field, but then perhaps it's all in the mind!

The anti-sterility vitamin is another name sometimes given to vitamin E, following the discovery that laboratory animals were unable to reproduce properly when the vitamin was lacking in their diet. Female animals suffered from repeated miscarriage, while male animals became sterile. A similar function for vitamin E in humans has yet to be proven, although the vitamin does appear to play some essential part in normal reproduction.

ALL IN A GOOD CAUSE

It has been said that women will go to almost any length to improve their looks, and in the case of vitamin E this certainly seems to be true. Some years ago in America it was discovered that when applied externally the vitamin would minimize wrinkles, scar tissue and stretch marks.

Soon, women all over the country were using their vitamin E capsules for a new purpose – squeezing out the sticky, fishy smelling oil and smearing it on their skin. Fortunately, today those who want to use vitamin E for this purpose no longer have to resort to such drastic measures since creams and lotions containing the vitamin are now widely available.

While on the subject of vitamin E's cosmetic properties, it is worth noting that even the most severe of burns has healed with scarcely a trace when vitamin E ointment has been applied regularly. Such treatment needs to begin straight away, since little improvement will be seen in an old scar.

OTHER ROLES OF VITAMIN E

The familiar symptoms of the menopause, such as hot flushes, depression, sweating, fear and nerves have been diminished with an increased intake of this vitamin.

Insufficient vitamin E in the diet may give rise to a form of anaemia with almost identical symptoms to those of iron deficiency anaemia. This may occur at any age, but has been found to be particularly common among bottle-fed babies.

Two functions of the vitamin particularly relevant to today are that vitamin E is also believed to protect the lungs from air pollution, and to reduce the side effects of such pain relieving drugs as codeine and morphine.

HOW MUCH TO TAKE

The premise that if a little does you good, a lot will do you even more good could prove dangerous in the case of vitamin E. Although the vitamin has no known toxic effect, even in large quantities, it could do more harm than good to some people.

For instance, anybody suffering from heart or circulatory troubles might be tempted to take large quantities of the vitamin to help restore their health. But those who have high blood-pressure, or who are diabetic, should take care, since large doses of vitamin E may simply aggravate these conditions.

The answer seems to be to start out with a small daily intake (say 100-200 i.u.'s), increasing the amount gradually if no side-effects occur. The Canadian doctors, Evan and Wilfrid Shute, who have worked extensively with vitamin E, have treated 30,000 cases of heart disease successfully, so there certainly seems to be something to be said for this form of therapy. (The doctors administered amounts ranging from 300 to 2,400 i.u.'s daily to their patients).

Although there is as yet no recommended minimum daily intake for this vitamin, a figure in the region of 100-400 i.u.'s has been suggested by many nutritionists. Dr Evan Shute believes that the average man should get a daily 600 i.u.'s and the average woman 400 i.u.'s. It is not considered advisable to exceed 1,600 i.u.'s daily for long periods just in case toxicity occurs.

If your diet contains plenty of vitamin E, you need not worry as much about your vitamin A intake. This is because adequate quantities of vitamin E allow greater storage of vitamin A, thereby reducing the requirement for this vitamin.

The most recent research suggests that a trace element called selenium is in some way connected with vitamin E. Selenium is not only one of the most powerful antioxidants known, but it also seems to increase the efficiency and effectiveness of vitamin E in its various roles. Selenium is present in many unrefined foods (e.g. raw sugar and wholegrains) but is destroyed by food processing, and by cooking.

OBTAINING ENOUGH VITAMIN E

Like the other fat-soluble vitamins, vitamin E cannot be absorbed by the body unless fat and bile are also present in the intestine at the same time. It is therefore advisable to take any supplement with a meal containing some fat. Similarly, since iron destroys vitamin E, these two nutrients should not be taken in conjunction.

When purchasing a supplement of this vitamin you can easily tell whether or not it is made from natural sources. The chemical name for vitamin E is tocopherol. There are several tocopherols, although the most active and the most commonly used is alpha tocopherol. The words 'd-alpha tocopherol' on the label of a supplement denote that the vitamin is derived from natural sources. 'dl-alpha tocopherol', on the other hand, signifies that it is a synthetic vitamin.

How can you obtain vitamin E from the diet? The best sources are wheat germ, unprocessed vegetable oils, and unprocessed cereals. Smaller amounts of the vitamin are also to be found in leafy green vegetables, seeds, nuts, lettuce, tomatoes, carrots, egg yolk and meat.

While vitamin E is not harmed by normal cooking processes, it is frequently destroyed during food refining. For instance, when the germ of wheat is removed. This is because it is in the embryo of the wheat grain (only present in wholegrain products) that the vitamin E is contained.

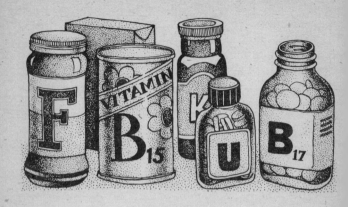

CHAPTER SEVEN

THE LESSER KNOWN VITAMINS

Because vitamins are a comparatively recent discovery, researchers are still unearthing new facts, both about established vitamins and about 'new' ones, and there is a good chance that we may still discover others.

We still have a lot to learn about all the vitamins, but this is especially true of those included in this chapter. Because so little is known about the vitamins described here, no recommended intake has yet been established for them.

VITAMIN P
Vitamin P is closely related to vitamin C, and the two are always to be found together in nature

(which is why a vitamin C supplement from natural ingredients is to be preferred to a synthetic one, which usually contains vitamin C in isolation).

Vitamin P is in fact another name for a group of eight substances called the bioflavonoids, of which the most active and the best known are rutin and hesperidin.

Little is known as yet about the precise role of vitamin P, but it appears to enhance the action of vitamin C, and to protect it in the body from destruction by oxygen. Vitamin P has been found to play a part in maintaining strong, healthy blood capillaries, thereby assisting the body in warding off infections.

This vitamin is present in fresh fruits, and is especially rich in citrus fruits, where it is concentrated in the pith and pulp of the fruit. So next time you painstakingly remove all traces of white pith from your orange, remember that this is where most of the vitamin P is to be found. Other good sources of this vitamin are rosehips, buckwheat, blackcurrants and grapes but, as with vitamin C, vitamin P is partially destroyed by water and cooking.

VITAMIN F

Like vitamin P, vitamin F has a 'partner' in nature – it is always to be found in conjunction with vitamin E, which protects it from oxidation. Vitamin F is better known as the polyunsaturated fatty acids, of which there are three: linoleic acid, linolenic acid, and arachidonic acid.

A lack of vitamin F in the diet is characterized

by such skin and hair complaints as eczema, dry skin, dry brittle hair, dandruff, boils and acne. This is because the vitamin serves to nourish the skin, but it also has a vital role to play in lowering cholesterol levels (cholesterol is the fatty substance which accumulates in the arteries, leading to strokes and cardiovascular diseases).

At the same time, vitamin F plays a part in maintaining the health of the cell membranes, the covering of the nerves, the thyroid gland and the kidneys. This is why it is extremely unwise to exclude all fat from the diet, as is the case with some strict slimming régimes.

Vitamin F is difficult to obtain from the diet, since it is present only in unprocessed cereal and vegetable oils (hence the emphasis on eating these as a means toward lowering cholesterol levels). Processing and hydrogenation (hardening) of oils destroy vitamin F, either because it is removed to prevent the oils from going rancid through oxidation, or because synthetic anti-oxidants are added which prevent the body from utilizing vitamin F. However, supplements of this vitamin are now available.

VITAMIN K
This is a fat soluble vitamin which derives its name from the word 'koagulation', the Danish spelling of the word, since it was discovered in that country.

Coagulation, or clotting of the blood, appears to be vitamin K's sole function and, in cases of deficiency, haemorrhaging occurs. Limited stores of the vitamin are maintained in the liver, where it is needed to help form prothrombin, a constituent of blood which produces clotting.

A deficiency of this vitamin is unlikely, since it is well distributed in green plants (especially spinach), with smaller quantities being present in soya beans, unrefined cereals, tomatoes, honey, bran, egg yolk and wheat germ. Added to this, a small amount of vitamin K can be produced by bacteria in the intestines provided the unsaturated fatty acids are present.

If a deficiency does occur, this is likely to be the result of taking drugs, or of a disorder of the liver which may interfere with the absorption or utilization of vitamin K.

It is common practice these days to administer vitamin K during childbirth since newborn babies cannot usually manufacture the vitamin, and there is therefore a danger of haemorrhage. A similar danger with the use of anti-coagulant drugs means that vitamin K is sometimes given to patients taking these drugs.

Like the other fat-soluble vitamins, vitamin K can be destroyed by freezing, by mineral oils and rancid fats. However, it is fairly resistant to heat and normal cooking processes.

VITAMIN B15

Vitamin B15, or Pangamic Acid as it is also known, was discovered in America, although the only countries in which it is currently used to any extent are Russia and Germany.

In the Soviet Union this vitamin is widely acclaimed as an aid to circulatory and heart troubles, too high cholesterol levels, skin problems, emphysema, and premature ageing. This is because the vitamin appears to supply oxygen to the body cells and the heart, while also acting as a detoxicant.

Vitamin B15, like the other members of the B complex, is water soluble. It is found principally in whole grains, brewer's yeast, brown rice, seeds, and apricot kernels.

VITAMIN B17

Vitamin B17, part of the nitriloside family, has been unofficially used in America in the chemical form known as laetrile for the treatment of cancer, and there are many claims of success. However, such treatment is only in the experimental stages, and is the subject of much controversy. The U.S. government has so far declined to give the vitamin official recognition, but there is a powerful popular movement to get the medical establishment to accept laetrile's alleged value in the battle against cancer. Vitamin B17 is found in kernels of most fruits, and especially apricot kernels, and it is a substance which clearly calls for a lot more research.

VITAMIN U

This vitamin has not been isolated chemically, but is a substance found in raw cabbages, large amounts of which have been found to help those suffering from ulcers. The same substance has also been identified in celery, raw milk, uncooked greens and raw egg yolk, but no traces of the vitamin have been found as yet in cooked foods.

CHAPTER EIGHT

VITAMINS FOR BEAUTY

The way you look is closely related to the state of your health, so it is perhaps not surprising that vitamins are as essential to your appearance as they are to your health.

Before you can even begin to improve your looks, you need first to acquire the bright eyes, clear complexion and silky shining hair which are only possible when the diet contains sufficient nutrients. A diet rich in the 'beauty vitamins' will have a more dramatic effect on your appearance than will any of the cosmetic concoctions on the market.

Apart from making sure your diet contains ample vitamins, you can also use these valuable substances in another way to enhance your appearance. Vitamins can be applied externally to the skin, where they will help to nourish the tissues and improve the circulation.

Most popular in this respect is undoubtedly vitamin E which, as already mentioned in Chapter 6, has the apparent ability to minimize wrinkles, scar tissue and stretch marks. Cosmetics with the added bonus of vitamin E now range from shampoos and soaps to moisturizers and facial mud packs.

If you prefer, you can add vitamin E (or any of the other vitamins) to your favourite cosmetics, simply by piercing a capsule and mixing the contents into the cream or lotion. A more potent form of vitamin E can be obtained by using the contents of the capsule 'neat', but this has the disadvantage of being rather heavy and cloying – as well as having a distinctly fishy smell.

For those who fancy trying their hand at making their own cosmetics, here is a recipe for a moisturizer with added vitamins. As you will see, it takes a little time and trouble to prepare, but at least you will know just what you are putting on your skin, and you will have the satisfaction of having 'done it yourself'. Your chemist shop should be able to provide you with most of the ingredients.

$1\frac{1}{2}$ **tablespoonsful white wax**
1 dessertspoonful anhydrous lanolin
$1\frac{1}{2}$ **fl. oz. (45ml) almond oil**
$\frac{1}{4}$ **teaspoonful borax**
2 fl. oz. (60 ml) rosewater
a few drops tincture of benzoin
2 vitamin E capsules
2 vitamin A capsules

Heat the wax and lanolin in a double boiler (a heatproof bowl over a pan of hot water will do equally well). Slowly add the almond oil. Meanwhile gently heat the rosewater and borax in another pan until the borax has dissolved. Add this to the wax and beat with an electric beater (or an untiring arm!) until the mixture cools to room temperature. Add the remaining ingredients and mix thoroughly. Store in an airtight container, and keep in a cool place.

IF AT FIRST YOU DON'T SUCCEED ...

Natural methods of healing are sometimes described as being 'safe but slow'. They do produce results, and without unwanted side-effects, but they do take time to have any effect. The same is true of vitamins when used in beauty therapy. Any benefit from applying vitamins to the skin is only likely to be derived from regular use over a prolonged period of time – so don't expect any overnight improvement!

BEAUTY FROM THE INSIDE

When taken internally, in the form of natural supplements or vitamin-rich foods, each of the vitamins has a part to play in improving your appearance.

Vitamin A, for instance, helps improve the condition of the hair and the eyes, and dry skin and dandruff are two common symptoms of a deficiency. Vitamin A's role in protecting the body against infection, by maintaining the health of the mucous membranes, also means that a shortage may result in such common skin complaints as acne, whiteheads and blackheads.

Anybody planning a holiday in the sun would be well advised to step up their intake of vitamin A for a few weeks before setting off, since this vitamin also has the ability to help the body build up protection to the burning rays of the sun. In normal circumstances this protection is built up too slowly to prevent burning, as many a sunbather will know to his or her cost!

The B vitamins help to control the skin secretions, and so help to achieve a balance in hair or skin that is either excessively dry or greasy. The B complex is especially important to the health of the hair, and a deficiency may result in poor growth or falling hair, dry and irritating scalp, dandruff and premature greying. Taking 200 mg of PABA after each meal for a period of six months is said to restore colour to grey hair in 70 per cent of cases, when accompanied by an increased intake of copper, folic acid and pantothenic acid.

Thread veins are an early indication that vitamin C is in short supply, since blood begins to seep from the fragile single cell capillaries to the surface of the skin. Since these veins are almost impossible to eradicate, this is one case where prevention is much better than cure. Vitamin C also helps to firm the skin tissue, and is important for the health of the hair, eyes and teeth.

Vitamin D's link with the minerals calcium and phosophorus make it essential not only for healthy bones, but also for strong teeth and nails. A deficiency is marked by nails that are soft and ridged, while dental decay is apparent.

Apart from its apparent ability to remove wrinkles and other skin blemishes, *vitamin E* also improves the circulation, which is a vital part of skin beauty. Brown 'age spots', or liver spots, which frequently appear on the backs of the hands, are also attributed to a lack of this vitamin.

CHAPTER NINE

WHAT VITAMINS DO YOU NEED?

Vitamin requirements vary from person to person, to the extent that two people who appear to have the same need (for example, identical height, weight and age), in fact have quite different requirements for certain vitamins.

This means, of course, that any table setting out vitamin requirements (such as that on page 91) can only give a very general indication of what you, as an individual, need. Such tables are worked out for the fictitious 'average man and woman', and in general indicate the minimum amount of a particular vitamin required to prevent the occurrence of deficiency diseases, plus a small safety margin. For instance, a daily intake of 20 mg of vitamin C is known to be sufficient in most cases to ward off scurvy – and the British recommended minimum intake of this vitamin is 30 mg daily.

ASSESSING YOUR REQUIREMENTS

If such vitamin charts are to be treated only as a guide, how then do you work out your own requirements of the various vitamins? Simply because each individual varies in his needs, there can be no hard and fast rules. It is really a matter of trial and error to find the optimum amount of each vitamin to maintain you at the peak of health.

Vitamin requirements are influenced by such factors as height, weight, age, amount of exercise and activity, how much sleep you get, and how much stress and worry you have to cope with. There are certain times and conditions, however, under which a person's requirement for certain vitamins increases. Such occasions are not, as you might think, few and far between, but are likely to affect any one of us during the normal course of everyday life. If you check the list below you will undoubtedly find that you fall into at least one of the 'special need' categories.

Slimming: Anybody who is trying to lose weight would be well advised to keep a check on his or her vitamin intake, since cutting down on calories invariably means cutting down on vitamins too. The fat soluble vitamins (A, D, E, and K) are especially likely to be in short supply, since most slimming diets restrict the amount of fat consumed. Boost your vitamin intake by eating plenty of fresh, raw fruit and vegetables, and add a few teaspoonsful of unsaturated vegetable oil to your diet.

The pill: The contraceptive pill, so widely used these days, depresses the levels of vitamins B6, B2 C, folic acid and B12, so increasing the body's need for these vitamins. Depression, which often occurs as a side-effect in women taking the pill has been linked with a deficiency of vitamin B6 Experiments in which 25 mg of the vitamin were administered daily to women suffering from such depression had a very high success rate. For those who are on the pill, supplements are now available to supply those nutrients which are likely to be lacking.

Drugs: The contraceptive pill is not the only drug to deplete the body's vitamin levels. The majority of medicines in common use today have a similar effect, and those vitamins most likely to be concerned are B6, C and folic acid. The vitamins are destroyed by antibiotics, while the use of mineral oil as a laxative destroys the fat soluble vitamins A, D, E and K.

Alcohol: Anybody who drinks regularly whether it be a little or a lot, is likely to be short of the B vitamins, since alcohol interferes with the body's absorption of these vitamins. Vitamin B1 is the most severely affected.

Eating out: If you eat out frequently – and this applies as much to *haute cuisine* establishments as it does to the local café – you may well be going short of some vitamins. This is because mass cooking methods and devices for keeping food hot are vitamin destroying, and the water-soluble C and B vitamins suffer most in this respect. The answer is to choose your menu carefully, opting for simple meals such as home-made soups, grills and salads, followed by fresh fruit or cheese.

Smoking: It is not just your lungs which are likely to suffer if you smoke. Cigarettes also lower the levels of vitamins B1 and C, and each cigarette you smoke is said to use up 25 mg of vitamin C – almost the equivalent of the British recommended daily intake. Another good reason for giving up the habit!

Athletes and the energetic: Those who indulge in strenuous physical exercise have an increased requirement for all the vitamins, because all that expended energy burns up extra vitamins just as it burns up extra calories.

Stress: There are many different forms of stress, but any kind increases the body's need for vitamins, especially the B and C vitamins. Illness, fear, extremes of temperature, and mental tension can all be classed as different types of stress. Mental stress can sometimes be prevented or alleviated by an increased intake of the B vitamins.

Pregnancy and breast-feeding: At no stage in a woman's life is her need for vitamins greater than at this vital time, for the obvious reason that she is providing nourishment both for herself and for her developing child. In particular demand are increased supplies of folic acid and vitamin B6. Folic acid is often prescribed as a matter of course to pregnant women (along with iron), since it helps to prevent haemorrhage and miscarriage, premature birth and complicated labour. That bane of pregnancy, morning sickness, often yields to a daily intake of 250 mg of vitamin B6, which also helps to counteract anaemia and oedema, both common complaints during pregnancy.

Old age: As one grows older, so all the body processes slow down and food is less well utilized than it once was. Extra vitamins are therefore needed to compensate for this. Old people who don't get out much are especially likely to be short of vitamin D as the vitamin is poorly distributed in food, and unless sufficient fresh fruit and vegetables are included in the diet there will also be a shortage of vitamin C. A survey conducted in Ireland among old people showed that 36 per cent were short of vitamin C. Taking a multi-vitamin supplement every day should help to counteract any such deficiencies.

CHAPTER TEN

CUTTING YOUR LOSSES

There is no room for complacency when considering vitamins. You may be eating a diet which, to all intents and purposes, is full of all the vitamins you need, only to find that many of these nutrients are being destroyed in the preparation and cooking of your food.

Most of the vitamins – the water-soluble ones in particular – are extremely unstable, and can be destroyed in any of several different ways. Just check through the following list, and see how many of these destructive factors your food is subjected to.

Air: Exposure to air destroys vitamins A and C in particular. This occurs when food is cut up and then left to stand around.

Light: Vitamins A, C and B all suffer throug exposure to light. Sunlight is particularl destructive.

Storage: Some vitamins are lost as soon as crop are harvested, and this 'leakage' continue throughout storage. Storing food in a freezer less destructive than other forms of storage provided the temperature is kept below –18°￼ (0°F). Foods must be quick frozen to retain the nutrients, and blanching food prior to freezin destroys thiamine and vitamin C (25 per cent an between 10 and 50 per cent respectively in th case of peas). Although most books on the subje recommend blanching (to preserve the food's fu colour) this stage can be missed out if foods a only to be stored for a relatively short period ￼ time, e.g. not much more than six months.

Water: Soaking and cooking foods in wat leaches out vitamins. In the case of many canne foods, only 40 per cent of the water solub vitamins are retained, and 20 per cent of th figure is to be found in the liquid in the can.

Heat: Heat such as that generated during th normal course of cooking destroys sever vitamins, but those most severely affected a thiamine and vitamin C. For instance in baking per cent of thiamine is lost, a figure whic increases to 30 per cent if a raising agent is use In the case of bread, if you then go on to ma toast, a further 15 per cent of thiamine is lost fro thick slices, or double that amount from th slices. Green vegetables may lose up to 70 p cent of their vitamin C content during cookin and this loss is further increased if foods are th kept hot. After half-an-hour of being kept hot, cabbage retains only 60 per cent of the vitamin C it had when just cooked, and this may fall to 40 per cent after a further half hour. Heat also activates enzymes which further destroy vitamins, although these enzymes are themselves destroyed by boiling water.

Food processing: Apart from losses incurred during cooking, food processing is probably responsible for more vitamin destruction than any other factor. Different vitamins are lost depending on the process used, but taking an everyday example such as milk, the following losses occur during processing:

Pasteurizing: 10 per cent thiamine; 20 per cent vitamin C

Sterilizing: 30 per cent thiamine; 50 per cent vitamin C

Evaporating: 20 per cent thiamine; 60 per cent vitamin C

Condensing: 5-10 per cent thiamine; 15 per cent vitamin C

In the case of flaked or puffed breakfast cereals there is a total loss of thiamine during manufacture.

Peeling: Peeling fruit and vegetables, especially prior to cooking, loses vitamins since these are often concentrated just under the skin. For instance, potatoes boiled after peeling lose 30-50 per cent of the vitamin C.

Alkali: The use of alkaline baking powder or bicarbonate of soda doubles losses of thiamine.

HOW TO CUT YOUR LOSSES

After reading through the above, you may begin to feel that there is no hope of obtaining all the vitamins you need from food, but it *is* possible to minimize vitamin losses in foods by adhering to certain guidelines. The way in which you purchase, prepare and cook your food can make all the difference to the vitamins you get from it. And although the following may sound at first like a laborious set of rules, you will find that it quickly becomes a habit.

1. Choose foods carefully, always buying them as fresh as possible. In the case of fruit and vegetables, the darker the colour, the higher the vitamin content.

2. Use as much of the fruit or vegetable as you can. The outer leaves of vegetables like cabbage and lettuce are the richest part of the plant, and can be incorporated in soups or stews, if not served as a vegetable. The outer leaves of lettuce for instance, can contain up to 30 times as much vitamin A as the heart.

3. Avoid buying processed foods as far as possible. Instead, choose whole, unrefined foods. Remember that frozen foods retain more nutrients than do those which are tinned or dehydrated.

4. Store food for as short a time as possible, both before and after cooking. Most fruit and vegetables are best if stored at 0°C (32°F), i.e. in the fridge or a cool cupboard. Cooked vegetables kept in the fridge for two or three days and then

eheated retain only between 33 and 50 per cent
s much vitamin C as they had when first cooked.

. Chop up food and cook straight away, to avoid
osses incurred by soaking or by exposure to air
nd light. Don't cut up food too small – this
ncreases vitamin losses since a larger surface area
exposed to air and light. Where foods must be
hopped in advance, such as for salad or fruit
alad, adding lemon juice or vinegar creates an
cid medium which protects vitamin C.

. Use the minimum amount of water in cooking
oods such as vegetables do not need to be
overed), and use up the cooking liquid
fterwards in a drink, casserole or soup. Steaming,
n which foods are placed over rather than in
ater, is even better.

Minimize enzyme destruction by plunging
oods straight into boiling water rather than
lowing them to heat through in the water.

Avoid the use of bicarbonate of soda to
nprove the colour of green vegetables, and add
lt, if required, at the end of the cooking time.

Cook food for the shortest time possible.
egetables should retain some firmness and
ould not be soggy and waterlogged.

). Avoid peeling fruit and vegetables before
ooking. Where possible the skins should be
ten too for extra roughage and nutrients. If you
e making a dish such as mashed potato, peel the
otatoes after cooking to minimize the loss of
tamin C.

11. Store foods out of light, especially avoidin sunlight. Steer clear of products bottled in cle; glass, such as orange juice, which will have lo; some of its vitamin C content while sitting on th shop shelf.

12. When using frozen foods, cook straight fror frozen where possible, or you can lose up to 5 per cent of the vitamin C content during th thawing process.

13. Pressure cooking has been found to minimiz the loss of vitamins for three reasons. These ar that cooking time is greatly reduced; a minimur amount of water is needed and the food is nc immersed; and no oxidation occurs. For instanc; potatoes cooked in this way were found to retai 79 per cent of their vitamin C and 100 per cent c their thiamine, compared with a retention of 7 per cent and 88 per cent respectively whe ordinary cooking methods were used.

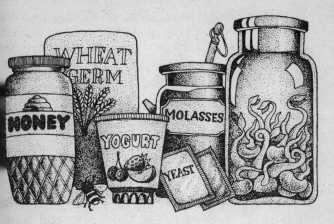

CHAPTER ELEVEN

VITAMINS FROM THE DIET

Vitamins are present in varying amounts in all foods, but there are certain dietary items which are especially rich in these nutrients. Such foods can easily be added to the daily diet to increase the intake of vitamins from natural sources. This chapter will introduce you to a few of these foods, with advice on how to add them to your diet.

BREWER'S YEAST FOR B VITAMINS

Brewer's yeast is one of the best and cheapest foods, being not only a complete protein but also the best non-animal source of all the B vitamins except B12 (which is often added by the manufacturer). This yeast was originally a by-product of the brewing industry (hence its name), but it is now produced specifically as a food.

Available in either tablet or powder form, the yeast's strong and rather unpalatable flavour is best disguised in drinks, soups, stews or cereals. Brewer's yeast should be taken only in small quantities at first, gradually increasing the amount to one tablespooonful daily, since it can otherwise make you feel rather bloated. This is only temporary, and suggests that the body was indeed in need of extra B vitamins.

A vitamin rich drink containing yeast can be made as follows:

$\frac{1}{2}$ **cupful fresh fruit of your choice (or fresh fruit juice)**
2 tablespoonsful vegetable oil
1-2 cupsful milk
$\frac{1}{2}$ **cupful powdered milk**
$\frac{1}{2}$ **cupful brewer's yeast**
1 teaspoonful vanilla essence

Put all the ingredients in an electric blender and blend until smooth. Add two more cupsful of milk and mix well. Start off with a quarter of a cupful of this drink at each meal, working up to two or more glasses a day. The drink will keep for up to two weeks if stored in the fridge.

THE VALUE OF WHEAT GERM
Wheat germ is the embryo from which the wheat plant develops, and as such it contains all the nutrients essential for growth. In this 2 per cent of the grain are concentrated rich supplies of vitamin E, most of the B vitamins, unsaturated oil, protein, and several minerals, especially iron.

Although wheat germ is present in the whole

grain and in products made from it (e.g. wholemeal flour), refining removes it from the grain. Food refiners are anxious to remove the germ because its high oil content will shorten the product's shelf life.

Wheat germ as a food comes in a finely flaked form, and is usually one of three types – unstabilized, stabilized, or toasted. When stabilized it has improved keeping properties, but it also contains less protein and fat and more carbohydrate than the unstabilized germ. You can toast wheat germ yourself by spreading it on a baking tray and cooking at gas mark $\frac{1}{2}$/121°C (250°F) until lightly browned. Unstabilized wheat germ should not be kept for more than two or three weeks once the packet has been opened, since it easily goes rancid.

Wheat germ has a mild nutty taste and can be incorporated in the diet in hundreds of ways. Sprinkle it on cereals, add it to casseroles, soups or drinks (it's delicious with fruit juice and yogurt), or include it in recipes for bread, biscuits or cakes. Wheat germ makes an excellent substitute for breadcrumbs as a topping or a covering for meat or fish. It is also delicious when eaten with honey and milk or yogurt as a quick and nourishing breakfast dish.

A NUTRITIOUS SWEETENER

Molasses is a residual syrup obtained during the sugar refining process. Successive boilings separate the pure sugar from this syrup, which contains the goodness of the original sugar cane in concentrated form, and with very little sugar.

Molasses is rich in vitamins of the B group, especially B1, B2, B6, pantothenic acid, choline and niacin. At the same time, it is an excellent source of many minerals, principally iron.

Molasses is a thick black syrup similar in texture and taste to treacle, although it has a more bitter flavour. There are various grades of molasses, the lighter coloured grades containing more sugar and therefore having a less strong taste.

Molasses may be used as a nutritious alternative to sugar in baking, where if necessary its flavour can be modified by mixing it half-and-half with honey. Molasses can also be used on its own as a spread, mixed in drinks, or taken in capsule form. It is especially recommended for relief of constipation, rheumatism, and anaemia.

Molasses used in gingerbread instead of the usual treacle imparts a much richer flavour, and is better for you too. Here is an easy recipe to try:

4 oz. (120 g) margarine
6 oz. (180 g) molasses
2 oz. (60 g) honey
¼ pint (150 ml) milk
2 eggs
8 oz. (230 g) wholemeal plain flour
1 level teaspoonful mixed spice
2 level teaspoonsful ground ginger
½ level teaspoonful bicarbonate of soda
2 oz. (60 g) raw sugar

Grease and line a 7 inch cake tin. Warm the margarine, molasses, honey and milk together. Allow to cool slightly. Beat the eggs and add. Mix together the dry ingredients and pour in the liquid mixture, stirring thoroughly. Bake at the centre of the oven at gas mark 3/165°C (325°F) for 1-1¼ hours.

A DUAL PURPOSE FOOD

Lecithin is used principally for its ability to emulsify or break down fats (including cholesterol), thus helping to prevent a build up of fatty deposits in the body. It is an accumulation of such fatty substances in the arteries which frequently leads to heart attacks or strokes.

However, lecithin does contain most of the B-complex vitamins, as well as vitamins A and K. For nutritional purposes lecithin is derived from the soya bean, and it comes in a granular form which can be eaten with fruit, cereal or yogurt.

AN IMPRESSIVE LIST

No list of vitamin-rich foods would be complete without the inclusion of alfalfa, which just about contains the lot. This plant, of which the seed is usually used, is a good source of vitamins A, D, E, K, C, B1, B2, B6, B12, folic acid, niacin, pantothenic acid, inositol and biotin. It is an impressive list, but what is alfalfa and how do you use it?

The alfalfa plant originated in North Africa, and is now widely used in the United States, principally as animal fodder. But you can add alfalfa to your diet by sprouting the tiny seeds (see instructions below), and eating the sprouts when they are about 1½ inches long. They are delicious added to salads, used in vegetarian savoury dishes, or included in bread recipes.

GROWING YOUR OWN BEAN SPROUTS

While on the subject of sprouts, these are a must for any diet which aims to be rich in all the vitamins. When beans or grains are sprouted their vitamin content shoots up (in some cases by as much as 100 per cent), and such sprouts are a good source of vitamins A, B, C, E and K. Half a cupful of sprouts contains as much vitamin C as six glasses of fresh orange juice.

Sprouts are fun, and they are easy to grow. The most common beans for sprouting – and found almost universally in Chinese restaurants – are the small green mung beans, which you can buy at health food shops. Other types that are often used are any kind of dried bean or pea, or such grains as wheat, rye, oats or barley.

To sprout beans or grains all you need is to take a quantity of the seeds, remembering that they will swell and increase in bulk so that half a cupful is ample for two people. Soak the beans overnight, then drain the water off and place them in a jam jar, porcelain bowl, or other similar container. Cover and place in a dark warm place, rinsing and draining the beans twice a day with warm water. In a few days time the sprouts will be ready to eat – beans, when the shoots are 1-2 inches long, and grains when the shoot is about the same length as the grain itself. Try eating sprouts raw in salads, or cooked in a variety of dishes. The sprouts will keep for two to three days, or for about a week if kept in the refrigerator. The sprouts may also be frozen successfully.

PLANNING YOUR DAILY DIET

It is easy to read through a list of vitamin-rich foods, but it is perhaps not so simple to incorporate them into a daily diet. Here is a suggested basic menu which includes plenty of foods supplying a broad spectrum of vitamins. Note the emphasis on fresh fruit and vegetables, and the use of unrefined whole foods.

Breakfast:

    freshly squeezed fruit juice

    muesli served with wheat germ, fresh fruit and unsweetened yogurt

    wholemeal bread and honey

    milk or herb tea

Lunch:

    mixed vegetable salad with a dressing of yogurt and lemon juice, or cider vinegar and vegetable oil

    wholemeal bread and low fat cheese or lean meat

    fresh fruit

    fruit juice or herb tea

Supper:

    home-made soup

    egg or cheese dish, or meat or fish

    lightly cooked fresh vegetables

    fresh fruit salad or a fruit-based dessert

    decaffeinated coffee or herb tea.

CHAPTER TWELVE

MEGAVITAMIN THERAPY

The body needs vitamins only in very small amounts to maintain a state of good health, but in certain illnesses vitamin doses far larger than normal have been used as an effective form of treatment.

Megavitamin therapy, as it is commonly known, is a relatively recent form of treatment, and one which still excites considerable controversy. While orthodox medical opinion seeks to discredit it, others claim some spectacular results when massive doses of vitamins are used.

Such treatment is concerned with the therapeutic rather than the nutritional use of vitamins. It is based on the theory that if small doses of vitamins are capable of eliminating disease (such as scurvy, beri-beri etc.), larger doses or combinations of vitamins should effectively treat certain illnesses. Such treatment appears to be effective only in conditions arising as a result of a definite vitamin deficiency.

Vitamins are administered orally or by injection into the veins or muscles. Injecting the vitamins in this way means that they are better absorbed since they pass direct to the bloodstream, and therefore smaller quantities may be given. Once improvement has been achieved through megavitamin therapy, a smaller maintenance dose is usually given regularly to prevent recurrence of the complaint.

CAUTION IS NEEDED

Megavitamin therapy is becoming increasingly common in America, although it is scarcely used as yet in Britain. The subject needs approaching with some caution, not only because it is difficult as yet to separate fact from fiction (tests tend to be unofficial and on a comparatively small scale only), but also because self-medication with large doses of anything can prove harmful. Unless you can track down a sympathetic doctor or unorthodox healer, it is therefore unwise to experiment with this form of treatment.

Because vitamins A and D can prove toxic in large amounts, these vitamins are seldom used in megavitamin therapy. Large amounts of vitamin D have been used in the treatment of arthritis and porous bones (osteoporosis), but such treatment carries with it a risk of hardening of the blood vessel walls. Similarly, vitamin A is occasionally used in large quantities for the treatment of acne, but this is usually limited to a short period of only three or four weeks.

Large doses of vitamin E are not known to produce toxicity, but although this vitamin is sometimes included in megavitamin therapy for its antioxidant properties, it is the B and C vitamins which are most commonly employed in this context.

SPECTACULAR RESULTS

Niacin, or vitamin B3, in particular has produced some spectacular results when used in massive doses in the treatment of schizophrenics, alcoholics, mentally disturbed children and heart patients.

The first trials with megavitamins took place in the 1950s, when two Canadian doctors, Hoffer and Osmond, began experiments in the treatment of schizophrenia. They were prompted to use niacin since the symptoms of pellagra (a niacin deficiency disease) are markedly similar to those of schizophrenia. They therefore treated their schizophrenic patients with doses of niacin ranging from 3 to 30 grammes daily. This was accompanied by 3 grammes of vitamin C each day, since schizophrenics often show a greatly increased need for this vitamin.

Since those early days Dr Hoffer, who is the leader in the field of megavitamin therapy, has treated many thousands of schizophrenics in this way, and he claims a 70 to 80 per cent success rate.

Alcoholics have been found to derive a similar benefit from this treatment, when administered with 3 to 20 grammes of niacin, and half that amount of vitamin C. In American trials 3 out of 4 alcoholics responded to this treatment. At the same time, the therapy alleviated low blood sugar which is common in both schizophrenics and alcoholics.

In the course of his research with megavitamins, Dr Hoffer has found that some mentally disturbed children appear to suffer from a niacin deficiency disease. This exhibits itself in a variety of symptoms, such as hyperactivity, poor school performance, or an inability to maintain social relationships. Such children responded to prolonged treatment with niacin, vitamin C and other vitamins, a combination which was continued in a smaller dose after the initial improvement.

Heart patients, too, have been treated successfully with an average daily intake of 3 grammes of niacin, since this B vitamin has the ability to lower fat levels and to discourage the formation of blood clots.

Drug addicts suffering from withdrawal symptoms have also obtained relief when given large doses of niacin in combination with vitamins C, B12 and B6.

LARGE AMOUNTS OF VITAMIN C
Another proponent of megavitamin therapy is, of course, Linus Pauling of vitamin C fame. As described in Chapter 4, this Nobel prize-winning scientist believes that doses in the region of 2 grammes daily can both ward off and alleviate the symptoms of the common cold. In addition to this

he advocates a normal daily intake of one to two grammes, which is very much higher than the 30 milligrams recommended by the British authorities as a daily requirement.

Large quantities of vitamin C (1 gramme or more per day) often help in the treatment of allergies too. This is because vitamin C and histamine (a highly toxic allergen found in the blood of allergic people) destroy one another, so that an allergy increases the body's need for the vitamin. Vitamin C is also required by the adrenal glands whose cortisone hormones are the most effective anti-allergy hormones.

An American doctor who has spent 25 years investigating the use of vitamin C in the treatment of allergies and severe infections, hails this vitamin as being the perfect antibiotic. Dr Klenner has found that many severe infections respond quickly to injections of between 2 and 6 grammes of vitamin C, administered every four to eight hours. And for those who would (quite rightly) be dubious about ingesting such large quantities, the doctor claims to have treated patients with between 50 and 100 grammes of vitamin C, without them suffering any untoward side-effects.

RECOMMENDED DAILY INTAKES

Recommended daily intakes of vitamins in Britain and the
United States

Vitamin	Britain	United States
A	2,500 i.u. (1,250 i.u.)	5,000 i.u.
B_1	0.8–1.4mg (0.3–1mg)	1.5mg
B_2	1.3–1.7mg (0.4–1.2mg)	1.7mg
B_3	15–18mg (5–14 mg)	20mg
B_6	none	2mg
B_{12}	none	6mcg
Folic acid	none	0.4mg
Pantothenic acid	none	10mg
Biotin	none	0.3mg
C	30mg	60mg
D	100 i.u. (250 i.u.)	400 i.u.
E	none	30 i.u.

figures in brackets for children up to 12 years.

To provide sufficient of the full range of vitamins your diet
should contain the following vitamin-rich foods:

Eggs (especially the yolks); milk; fresh fruit and vegetables
(especially watercress, spinach, oranges); brewer's yeast;
wholegrains; wheat germ; liver; molasses; beansprouts;
unprocessed vegetable oils.

INDEX